577.34
PIPES

Pipes, Rose.

Rain forests

T 1822

RAIN FORESTS

Rose Pipes

Austin, Texas

Published by Raintree Steck-Vaughn Publishers,
an imprint of Steck-Vaughn Company

A ZOË BOOK

Editors: Kath Davies, Pam Wells
Design & Production: Sterling Associates
Map: Sterling Associates

Library of Congress Cataloging-in-Publication Data

Pipes, Rose.
Rain Forests / Rose Pipes.
p. cm. — (World Habitats)
"A Zoë Book"—T.p. verso.
Includes index.
Summary: Introduces some notable rain forests around the world, including those of South America, Congo, and Central America.
ISBN 0-8172-5003-4
1. Rain forests—Juvenile literature. 2. Rain forest ecology—Juvenile literature. [1. Rain forests.] I. Title. II. Series: Pipes, Rose. World habitats.
QH86.P57 1998
577.4—dc21 97-9070
CIP
AC

Printed in Italy
Bound in the United States
1 2 3 4 5 6 7 8 9 01 00 99 98 97

Photographic acknowledgments

The publishers wish to acknowledge, with thanks, the following photographic sources:

Britstock-IFA / West Stock 24; Environmental Images / C Jones 9; / Irene Lengui 21; Robert Harding Picture Library / Jennifer Fry 15; / K Gillham 23; The Hutchison Library / Adrian Clark 16; / Sarah Errington 17; Impact Photos / Colin Jones - title page, 14; / Clic Clap 7; / Guy Moberly 12; / Neil Morrison 18; NHPA / David Middleton 25; / Dr. Ivan Polunin 27; South American Pictures / Tony Morrison 7; Still Pictures / Yves Thonnerieux 5; / Mark Edwards 8, 10, 11; / Hellier Mason 13; / Klein/Hubert 20; / Thierry Montford 22; / Dario Novellino 26, 29; / Nigel Dickinson 28; TRIP / M Both 19; Zefa - cover background, insets tl & br.

Contents

All the words that appear in **bold** are explained in the Glossary on page 30.

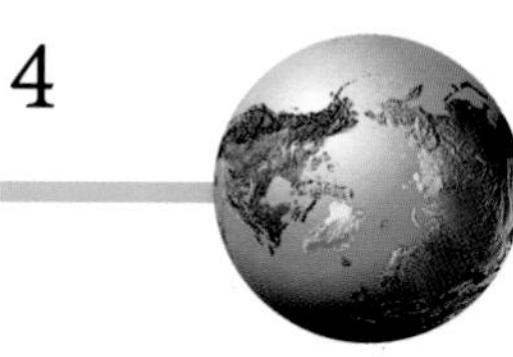

Where and What Are Rain Forests?

Most rain forests grow in places where it is hot and wet all year long. These are tropical rain forests.

Rain forests also grow in cooler places. These are temperate rain forests with a milder climate.

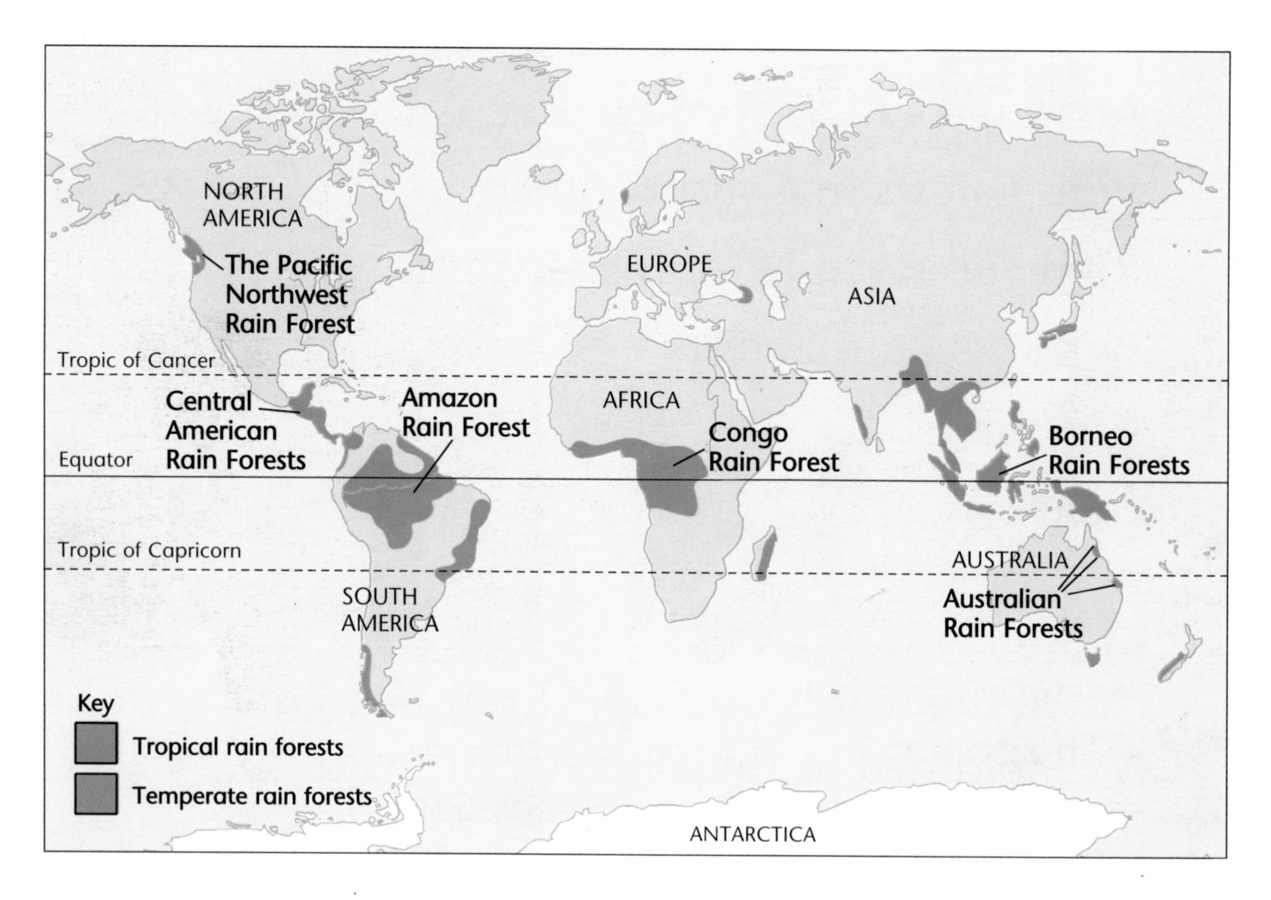

You can see all the world's rain forests on this map.

The trees in a rain forest are green all year. They grow close together. Their leaves and branches form a roof, or **canopy**, above the forest. Many animals live in the canopy because there is plenty of light and food here.

Below the canopy it is dark and damp. Hundreds of different plants grow among the trees. Some plants climb up the tree trunks or grow on tree branches, like the ones shown here.

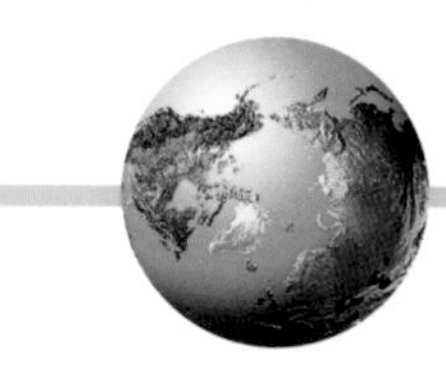

Life in the Rain Forests

More kinds of plants and animals live in the rain forest **habitat** than in any other habitat on earth.

Animals such as this gray woolly monkey are well adapted to living in tall trees. They use their long tails and arms to hold on to branches.

Many rain forest plants have brightly colored flowers. These flowers stand out from the green leaves that surround them. The color attracts birds and insects to come to feed on the **nectar** in the flowers.

People have lived in the rain forests for thousands of years. They know how to find food and the other things they need to survive in the forest.

A bird feeds on nectar from a plant, in Martinique, an island in the West Indies.

Rain Forests in Danger

Rain forest trees are cut down or burned every year. Many people believe this is changing the world's **climate**.

Rare animals and plants are dying out as well. Parts of some rain forests are now **preserves** where wildlife is kept safe for

People destroy thousands of trees and other plants to make roads like this one. Forest people lose their homes.

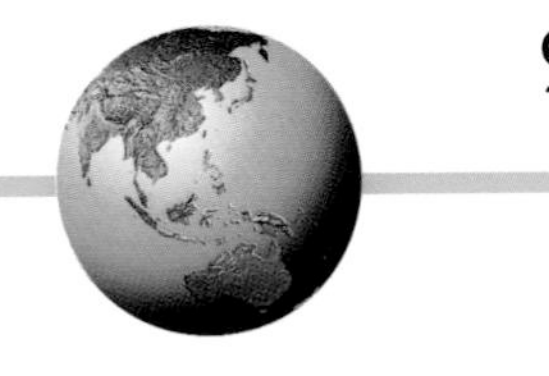

the future. The trees are protected too. A special plan that protects mahogany trees, is just one example.

Many useful plants grow in rain forests. There are nuts and fruit, and plants for making medicines. These are **natural resources**.

The wood from some trees, for example mahogany, is used for furniture. Other trees are used to make plywood and building materials.

Rubber trees grow wild in some tropical rain forests. This person is cutting a rubber-tree trunk to collect its sap. Rubber is made from the latex, or sap of the tree.

The Amazon Rain Forest in South America

The world's largest rain forest grows in South America. It crosses the boundaries of nine different countries. The great Amazon River flows through the center of the rain forest

People burn large areas of the forest to clear away the trees. Farmers keep cattle on most of this land. Some of the beef is sold to make hamburgers.

across the **continent** of South America.

Tin and gold are metals that are mined in the Amazon rain forest. Big machines clear away the trees and the soil. Then the metals are dug out. When it rains, the bare soil turns to mud and washes away easily. Mines like this one can destroy the forest and its wildlife forever.

This is a tin mine in the rain forest.

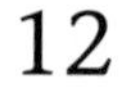

In an area of rain forest only 4 miles (6 km) square, there may be as many as 1,500 different types, or **species**, of plants, 400 species of birds, and 250 species of **mammals**.

Some of the forest animals, such as these macaws, live only in the Amazon rain forest. If people clear more forest, macaws may become **extinct**.

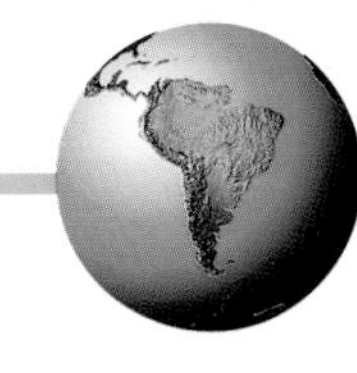

Many of the trees and plants can be used for medicines, for industry, and for food. People gather forest resources and sell them to countries around the world.

Harvesting forest resources in this way brings jobs for people. It also makes money for the rain forest countries. Unlike mining, it does not destroy the forest habitat.

These Brazil nuts are sold to make money for peoples of the rain forest. These people are sometimes called rain forest Amerindians.

The Rain Forest in Congo, Africa

Congo is a large country in Africa. Rain forest once covered most of the land. In the north, very little forest has been cleared. Few people live in this part of Congo.

The Congo River runs through the northern forest. Large boats cannot travel along the river because there are **rapids** like the ones shown here.

Congo has more kinds of mammals and birds than any other country in Africa. About 11,000 species of plants grow in Congo. Many of these plants do not grow anywhere else. Parts of Congo's rain forest are now **national parks**. People visit these parks to see the wildlife.

Mountain gorillas are very rare. There are only about 450 living in the wild. They died out because of hunting and because their habitat changed.

Many different forest peoples live in Congo. The Mbuti Pygmies live in the eastern part of the rain forest. They live in simple dome-shaped houses made from wood and leaves.

The Mbuti gather wood and leaves from the forest to build their houses.

The Mbuti are very skilled hunters. They hunt wild animals and gather forest plants. They can find all the food that they need in the forest.

The Mbuti travel outside the forest to **trade** with other people. They trade forest foods, such as bananas, fish, and honey. They exchange these for other goods, such as peanuts, knives, and cooking pots.

Mbuti hunters wait for food to be cooked.

Australia's Rain Forests

Australia's rain forests are in Queensland, on the northeast side of the continent. This is one of the wettest parts of Australia. There are three areas of rain forest on the coast.

The rain forests lie between the mountains and the coast. You can see the edge of the rain forest near this beautiful beach in Queensland.

People have cleared some of the rain forest. Near the coast, farmers grow **crops** such as sugarcane. On higher land there is grazing land for cattle.

Almost all the rain forest is now a United Nations World Heritage Site. This rain forest cannot be cleared, and the wildlife is safe for the future.

Koulmoon Creek is in the rain forest in the United Nations World Heritage Site.

Many unusual plants and animals live in the Australian rain forests. The tree kangaroo grips branches with its long tail and jumps from tree to tree on its strong back legs.

The tree kangaroo has long toes, and claws on its front feet help it to hold food.

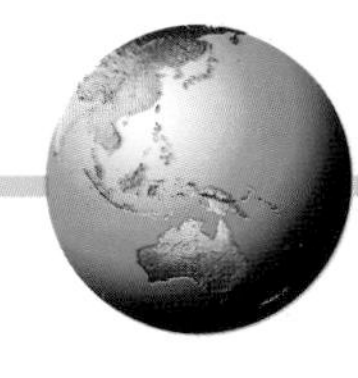

Australia's rain forests are famous for large butterflies and moths. The biggest butterfly has such wide wings it is called a birdwing butterfly.

Many tourists visit Australia's rain forests each year. Part of the rain forest is the Yarrabah Aboriginal Reserve. Tourists visit the preserve and Daintree National Park.

A boat trip on the Daintree River is a good way of seeing the forest and its wildlife.

Rain Forests in Central America

Tropical rain forest once covered nearly all of Central America. Most of the forest was cleared, but what is left is rich in wildlife. Rain forest peoples such as the Bribri still

Bribri hunt green iguana like this one. It is good to eat and is now bred for its meat.

hunt and gather food. They live in the southern part of the rain forests.

In Panama, where people have cleared the rain forest, there are no longer trees to hold the soil. Heavy rains wash the soil into the Panama Canal.

The soil builds up on the bottom of the canal. The water must be deep enough for big ships to sail through, so workers clear the soil from the canal.

A boat called a dredger is used to clear soil from the Panama Canal.

Rain Forests in North America

Temperate rain forest grows near the coast on the mountains of northwest America. Heavy rain falls here. Some of the largest trees in the world grow in this rain forest.

Bright green mosses grow on the floor of the temperate rain forest.

The Douglas fir can grow to be 200 feet (61 m) tall and 10 feet (3 m) wide.

In Washington State, the rain forest is now preserved in the Olympic National Park. There are trails in the park where tourists can walk.

Tourists come to the forest to enjoy the beautiful scenery. They may also see some of the wild animals that live in the forest.

Elk, a kind of deer, and marmots, small rodents, live in the park. Black bears live there too.

Borneo's Rain Forest

Rain forest once covered the island of Borneo in Asia. Today only about half the forest is left. Some of it burned down in forest fires, and some was cleared to make **plantations**. People grow rubber, cocoa, and coffee here.

These women are planting oil palm trees on a plantation. The oil is used to make many things, such as soap and shampoo.

Borneo's rain forest is the home of many rare animals and plants. Some, such as the Bornean bristlehead bird, are found nowhere else in the world.

More than 2,500 kinds of orchids grow in Borneo's rain forests. A climbing plant called rattan, which is used to make furniture, is grown here, too.

Orchids are beautiful flowering plants that grow on tree branches, like these in North Borneo.

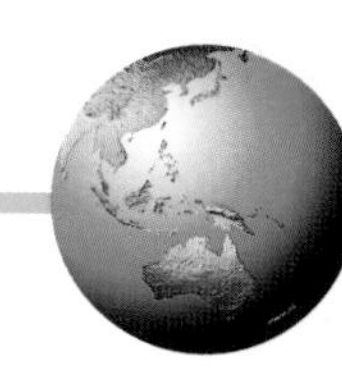

Some of the Penan of Borneo live in the forest. Many of these people now have small farms where they grow rice. But they still depend on the forest for food and other things. They hunt wild pigs and deer in the

This Penan man uses his blowpipe to hunt for food.

forest. They also gather honey and a plant called sago.

In many places it is easier to move logs on rivers than on land. The lumber is sold for building and furniture making.

Logging companies cut down trees on land where the Penan lived. The Penan **protested**, so parts of the forest were set aside for the people to live in.

These logs are being floated down the river to a **port**.

Glossary

adapted: If a plant or an animal can find everything it needs to live in a place, we say that it has adapted to that place. The animals can find food and shelter, and the plants have enough food in the soil and enough water. Some animals have changed their shape or their color over a long time, so that they can catch food or hide easily.

canopy: In a rain forest, the tops of trees are very close together. The branches and leaves form a roof, or canopy, above the forest.

climate: The type or pattern of weather in a particular place.

continent: One of the seven large landmasses in the world. They are Europe, Asia, North America, South America, Australia, Antarctica, and Africa.

crops: Plants that farmers grow to use or to sell.

extinct: When one type of animal or plant has died out forever, we call it extinct.

habitat: The natural home of a plant or an animal. Examples of habitats are deserts, forests, and grasslands.

mammals: Warm-blooded animals whose young feed on their mother's milk.

national parks: Laws protect these lands and their wildlife from harm.

natural resources: Things that are found in nature and are useful to people, such as wood from trees.

nectar: A sweet fluid made by plants in their flowers.

plantations: Farms that grow one kind of tree or crop. Tea, coffee, and rubber trees are grown on plantations.

port: A town where ships load and unload goods. Ports are next to rivers, lakes, or oceans.

preserve: An area safe from changes that would spoil or destroy it. A nature preserve is an area set aside for wildlife to live in.

protest: To argue against something.

rapids: A place where a river runs very fast over rocks or down a steep slope.

species: A group of plants or animals of the same type.

trade: To buy and sell, or to exchange, goods.

Index